*Written in 2020
Sylvan Lake,
Alberta, Canada.*

For Anastasia, Maverick, Alexandria and Remy.

Big thank you to Yvonne Spady for all your help and support!

illustrated by

Oswaldo Santaella & Nicolas Urquiola

You woke up today and on the TV,
were all these crazy stories about Covid-19.
You could see Mom and Dad had worry on their face.
Just remember, The Coronavirus isn't scary,
we just have to keep ourselves safe!

You head out to the market, there are arrows on the floor. You have to sanitize your hands when you come on through the door.

You're not to stand too close to others,
can't give as many hugs.
You can still say hello and smile
or give a simple wave.

The Coronavirus isn't scary,
We just have to keep ourselves safe.

You haven't been to Grandma's house,
or to your friends to play.
As long as we listen to the doctors,
everything will be okay!

You've had to cancel family trips. You can't travel too far from home. It won't be like this forever though, one day soon you'll be free to roam!

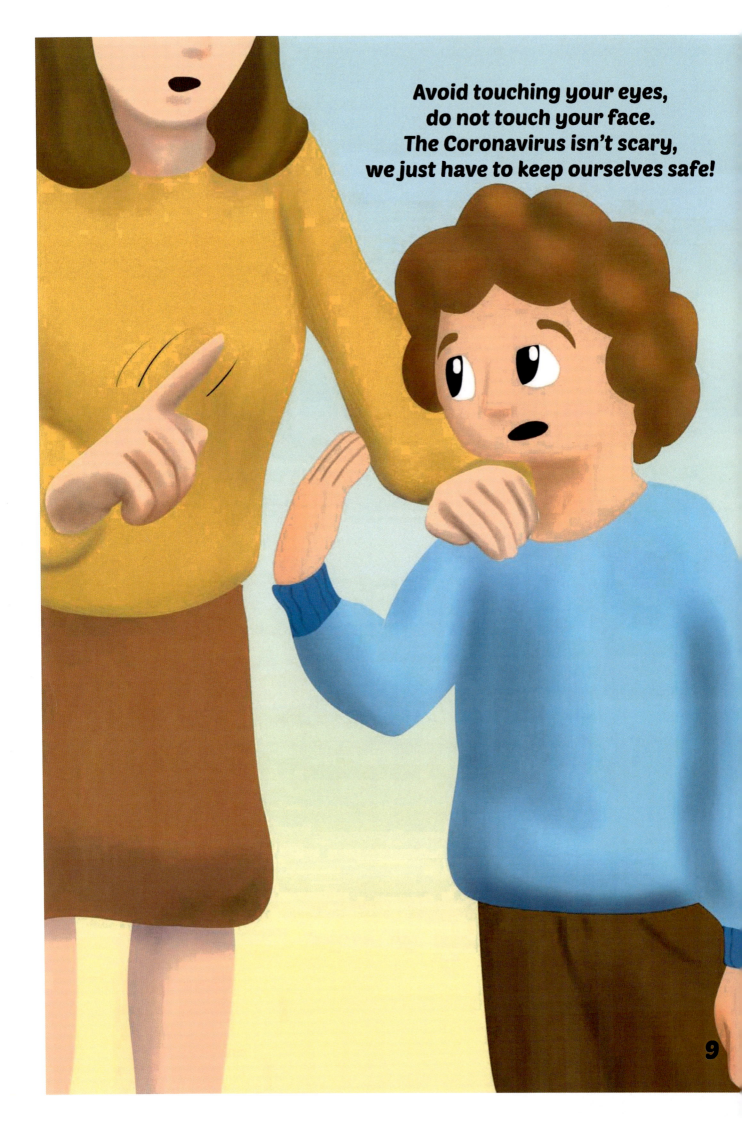

So when things are seeming odd,
and the world looks like a different place.
Just remember, The Coronavirus isn't scary,
we just need to keep ourselves,
SAFE!

Now it is your turn to color the pages!

Re-Read the story and add your own colors!

You woke up today and on the TV,
were all these crazy stories about Covid-19.
You could see Mom and Dad had worry on their face.
Just remember, The Coronavirus isn't scary,
we just have to keep ourselves safe!

You haven't been to Grandma's house, or to your friends to play. As long as we listen to the doctors, everything will be okay!

You've had to cancel family trips. You can't travel too far from home. It won't be like this forever though, one day soon you'll be free to roam!

So when things are seeming odd,
and the world looks like a different place.
Just remember, The Coronavirus isn't scary,
we just need to keep ourselves,
SAFE!

Keep yourself
Safe!!
—Kristy Walker

Keep yourself
Safe !!

—Julieta Walker

Made in the USA
Columbia, SC
01 February 2021